Famous Legends

The Legend of Sleepy Hollow

D1712547

By
Shalini Saxena

Gareth Stevens
PUBLISHING

Please visit our website, www.garethstevens.com. For a free color catalog of all our high-quality books, call toll free 1-800-542-2595 or fax 1-877-542-2596.

Cataloging-in-Publication Data

Saxena, Shalini.
The legend of Sleepy Hollow / by Shalini Saxena.
p. cm. — (Famous legends)
Includes index.
ISBN 978-1-4824-2752-3 (pbk.)
ISBN 978-1-4824-2753-0 (6 pack)
ISBN 978-1-4824-2754-7 (library binding)
1. Irving, Washington, — 1783-1859. — Legend of Sleepy Hollow — Juvenile literature. 2. Ghosts — New York (State) — Sleepy Hollow — Juvenile literature. 3. Sleepy Hollow (N.Y.) — Legends — Juvenile literature. I. Saxena, Shalini, 1982-. II. Title.
PS2067.S29 2016
133.109747'277—d23

First Edition

Published in 2016 by
Gareth Stevens Publishing
111 East 14th Street, Suite 349
New York, NY 10003

Copyright © 2016 Gareth Stevens Publishing

Designer: Laura Bowen
Editor: Therese Shea

Photo credits: Cover, p. 1 John Quidor/Wikimedia Commons; cover, p. 1 (ribbon) barbaliss/Shutterstock.com; cover, p. 1 (leather) Pink Pueblo/Shutterstock.com; cover, pp. 1–32 (sign) Sarawut Padungkwan/Shutterstock.com; cover, pp. 1–32 (vines) vitasunny/Shutterstock.com; cover, pp. 1–32 (parchment) TyBy/Shutterstock.com; cover, pp. 1–32 (background) HorenkO/Shutterstock.com; p. 5 (main) Science & Society Picture Library/SSPL/Getty Images; p. 5 (inset) Hulton Archive/ Getty Images; p. 6 DeCe/Shutterstock.com; pp. 7, 27 Dennis K. Johnson/Lonely Planet Images/Getty Images; pp. 9 (main), 13, 21, 23 Culture Club/Hulton Archive/Getty Images; p. 9 (inset) © iStockphoto.com/gkuchera; p. 10 Peter Pelham/ Wikimedia Commons; p. 11 DEA/G. DAGLI ORTI/De Agostini/Getty Images; p. 14 Darley/Wikimedia Commons; p. 15 © iStockphoto.com/JacobH; p. 17 (statue) John Rogers/Wikimedia Commons; p. 17 (garden) Unholy Vault Designs/ Shutterstock.com; p. 19 LEE SNIDER PHOTO IMAGES/Shutterstock.com; p. 22 Frederick Simpson Coburn/Wikimedia Commons; p. 24 F.O.C. Darley/Wikimedia Commons; p. 25 vectorbomb/Shutterstock.com; p. 29 (main) Everett Historical/ Shutterstock.com; p. 29 (inset) Anthony22/Wikimedia Commons.

Printed in the United States of America

CPSIA compliance information: Batch #CS15GS: For further information contact Gareth Stevens, New York, New York at 1-800-542-2595.

Contents

Words in the glossary appear in **bold** type the first time they are used in the text.

Beware!

On the eastern shore of the Hudson River in New York, there's a quiet village called Tarrytown. Many Dutch colonists settled there in the days before the **American Revolution**. Near the village is a valley with some woods and a stream. The place had a dreamy air, and so the area was called Sleepy Hollow.

But be warned. You don't want to walk alone in Sleepy Hollow at night. If you do, the Headless Horseman may get you! At least, that's how "The **Legend** of Sleepy Hollow" goes.

The Inside Story

Years after "The Legend of Sleepy Hollow" was first **published**, a town near Tarrytown named itself Sleepy Hollow.

"The Legend of Sleepy Hollow" is a short story by American writer Washington Irving (below). Tarrytown (called Tarry Town in Irving's story) is a real place.

5

A Rider in the Night

According to the legend, many spirits and **supernatural** figures **lurked** in Sleepy Hollow, but the scariest was the Headless Horseman. Every night, a body without a head rode through the area on horseback!

The Headless Horseman was said to be the ghost of a Hessian soldier who fought in the American Revolution. A cannonball had taken off his head. So, he rode from the graveyard where he was buried to the battlefield to look for his head. He then returned to the graveyard before dawn.

The body of the Hessian soldier was said to be buried in the graveyard of the Old Dutch Church in Sleepy Hollow, right next to the Sleepy Hollow Cemetery.

The Inside Story

Hessians were soldiers from an area called Hesse-Cassel in modern-day Germany. They helped the British fight the colonists during the American Revolution.

The Schoolmaster

According to Washington Irving, despite the shadowy figures of the night, life in Sleepy Hollow carried on normally during the day. It had one school and one schoolmaster, a man from Connecticut named Ichabod Crane. His name suited him—he looked a bit like the bird.

Ichabod was a firm but fair teacher. After school, he often played with the older boys. He also taught singing to people around town and helped townspeople with chores. Throughout the year, Ichabod lived with the families of different students.

The Inside Story

Ichabod was like many teachers in the early 1800s, doing extra work to make more money. Teachers often didn't have their own homes, so they stayed with students.

Ichabod Crane taught in a one-room schoolhouse, in which students of all ages would sit together. These schools were once very common, but now very few remain.

9

Ghost Stories

With all the strange tales surrounding Sleepy Hollow, it should be no surprise that many townspeople, including Ichabod, were **superstitious**. Still, they loved to share ghost stories and odd tales. Ichabod especially loved a book called *History of New England Witchcraft* by Cotton Mather.

In the evenings, Ichabod would sit around a fire with the wives of the town, sharing stories he knew about witchcraft. He would also listen to their tales of ghosts, haunted places, and the Headless Horseman.

The Inside Story

Cotton Mather (right) was a **minister** from Boston, Massachusetts. In the late 1600s, when he lived, people in Massachusetts were killed because they were believed to be witches.

Around a cozy fire, the ghost stories and creepy tales didn't seem so scary.

11

Into the Woods

For all his love of scary stories, Ichabod wasn't very brave. After he left the house he was visiting, he would make his way to the home where he was staying. His eyes would start playing tricks on him.

In the night, each bush looked like a ghost. Every burst of wind sounded like the howling of the Headless Horseman. The sound of his own footsteps on frost would make him jump. Even with all his knowledge, Ichabod could be rather fearful.

The Inside Story

The Headless Horseman is most likely based on the German legend of the Wild Huntsman. He rode on horseback chasing people guilty of terrible crimes.

To Ichabod, the woods seemed like a safe place during the day, but there was no telling what could happen at night.

13

The Farmer's Daughter

Even when daylight came, Ichabod was haunted. Not by ghosts, though—by a woman. The pretty Katrina Van Tassel was one of his singing students. She was the daughter of a rich farmer in the town, Old Baltus Van Tassel.

Katrina was good-looking, but the always-hungry Ichabod was really drawn to all the fine food he could eat if he married her and took over her family farm. Roasted pig, juicy ham, tasty sausages, and more would all be his!

It's said that many women liked to spend time with Ichabod, walking around this lake near Phillipsburg Manor, which still stands in Tarrytown. However, Ichabod only wanted to be with Katrina.

15

The Rival

Unluckily for Ichabod, there were many **rivals** for Katrina's love. Abraham, or Brom, Van Brunt was one of these. Because he was big and strong, people called him Brom Bones. When he began courting Katrina, other men were too scared to try—except for Ichabod.

Ichabod didn't want to fight with Brom, so he tried to win Katrina with sweet words and singing lessons. But Brom and his friends played dirty. They ruined Ichabod's schoolhouse and teased him in front of Katrina.

The Inside Story

In the early 1800s, if a man wanted to marry a woman, he would have to court her, or show her and her family that he would be a good husband if they married.

In many ways, Brom was the opposite of Ichabod. He was big, loud, and a bit of a bully, while Ichabod was thin, quiet, and kept out of trouble.

statue of Ichabod and Katrina

An Important Invitation

Katrina wouldn't choose between Brom and Ichabod, so their rivalry continued for a time. Then one fall day, while Ichabod was teaching, he received an invitation to a party at Baltus Van Tassel's farm. He grew very excited—a chance to win Katrina once and for all!

Ichabod went home to get ready. He wanted to fit in with the other guests, so he borrowed farmer Hans Van Ripper's horse, Gunpowder. The horse was old, slow, and a little small for Ichabod, but it didn't matter to him.

The Inside Story

Most believe Katrina Van Tassel and Brom Bones were partly named after and based on real people.

The real Katrina Van Tassel and Brom Bones are buried in Sleepy Hollow Cemetery.

19

A Grand Evening

When Ichabod arrived at the party, he saw tables of mouth-watering food. But music began to play, so Ichabod danced with Katrina. He was a very **clumsy** dancer, but he didn't know it. Brom was **jealous**. Ichabod was having too much fun to notice, though.

Later, guests started trading ghost stories. Ichabod told tales of witchcraft from Cotton Mather's book. People talked of seeing the Headless Horseman themselves. Brom bragged that he wasn't afraid of the Horseman, but others didn't feel quite as brave.

The Inside Story

In the stories of the Headless Horseman the townspeople told, he always disappeared before crossing the bridge near the church.

Ichabod believed he danced as well as he sang, but to other guests, he was a funny sight to see.

21

A Turn for the Worse

As the guests were leaving, Ichabod spoke with Katrina. He was certain he had finally won her. But it was not so. She had only spent time with Ichabod to make Brom jealous. Poor Ichabod left the house and rode into the dark woods outside.

His mind started to see **goblins** all around. He began to **whistle** to calm himself. But as he reached a bridge over a stream, his heart sank. This stream was said to be cursed. Suddenly, Ichabod noticed a large shape lurking nearby. The shape began to move.

Ichabod's ride home was much less cheerful than his ride to the party. Little did he know it would get even worse.

23

The Smashed Pumpkin

Ichabod saw that the shape was a headless rider—with his head in his hand! Ichabod began to race away on Gunpowder, but the Headless Horseman was right behind him. Ichabod thought he felt hot breath on the back of his neck. Soon, he was almost to the church bridge where he thought he'd be safe. Ichabod looked back. He saw the rider rise up and throw his head at him!

The next day, Ichabod was nowhere to be found. All that remained on the road was Gunpowder the horse and a smashed pumpkin.

Some TV shows and movies about this legend show the Horseman's head as a **jack-o'-lantern** on fire.

25

The End of Ichabod

Ichabod Crane was never seen in Sleepy Hollow again. Many believed the Headless Horseman had carried him away. Or had he? One townsman had heard that Ichabod Crane had moved because he was upset about Katrina and the happenings of that night.

A strange thing happened whenever someone told the story of Ichabod around Brom Bones. Brom, who married Katrina, would smile and burst into laughter when he heard about the broken pumpkin. Maybe, just maybe, there was more to the story.

The Inside Story

Ichabod Crane was named after a real person Washington Irving had met. However, the real Ichabod was a soldier.

Although the bridge Ichabod Crane tried to cross is now long gone, visitors like to go to this one near the Sleepy Hollow Cemetery.

27

America's First Ghost Story

There are many cartoons, TV shows, and movies about Ichabod Crane and the Headless Horseman. However, the original short story, "The Legend of Sleepy Hollow," was first published in Washington Irving's *The Sketch Book* in 1819 and 1820. It was America's first ghost story.

Washington Irving wasn't only looking to scare his readers. He wanted to make them laugh. Ichabod's silly dancing was just one funny part. Readers loved both the funny and scary parts of the story. And even now, people still love to imagine what really happened in Sleepy Hollow.

The Inside Story

Washington Irving also wrote the short story "Rip Van Winkle" about a man who falls asleep for 20 years.

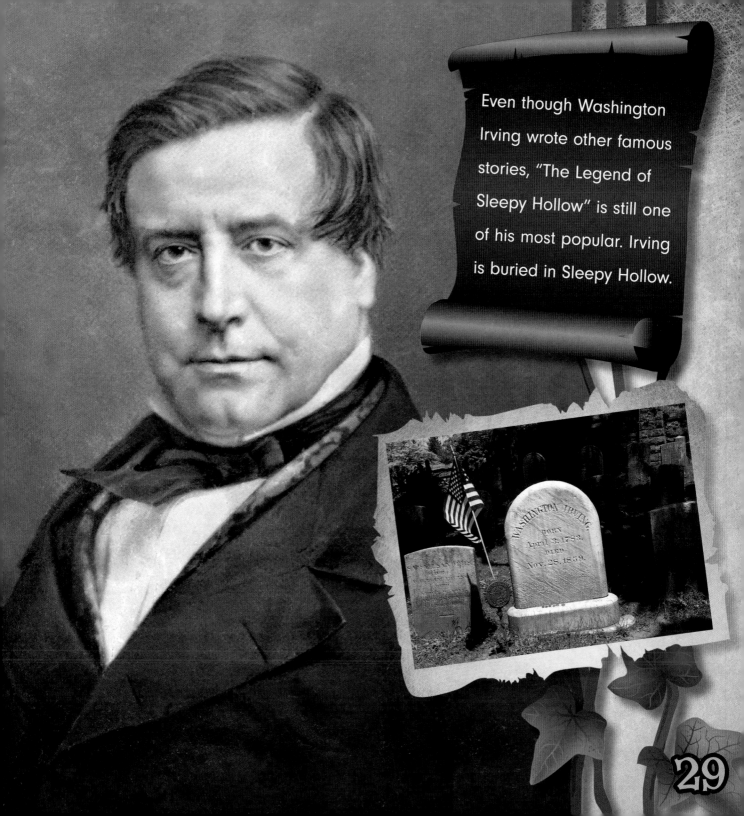

Even though Washington Irving wrote other famous stories, "The Legend of Sleepy Hollow" is still one of his most popular. Irving is buried in Sleepy Hollow.

29

Glossary

American Revolution: the war in which the colonies won their freedom from England (1775–1783)

clumsy: not moving easily or smoothly

goblin: an ugly and sometimes evil creature in stories that likes to cause trouble

jack-o'-lantern: a pumpkin that has had its insides removed and a face cut into it for Halloween

jealous: feeling unhappy or angry because of someone's attention to another person

legend: a story that has been passed down for many, many years that's unlikely to be true

lurk: to wait in a secret or hidden place especially in order to do something wrong or harmful

minister: a person who leads a church service

publish: to produce material in print for sale

rival: a person who tries to be more successful than another person

supernatural: unable to be explained by science or the laws of nature

superstitious: believing in the unknown and having faith in magic or luck

whistle: to make a sound by blowing breath through lips or teeth

For More Information

Books

Cocca, Lisa Colozza. *Sleepy Hollow*. New York, NY: PowerKids Press, 2015.

Hoena, Blake A., and Tod Smith. *Washington Irving's The Legend of Sleepy Hollow: A Graphic Novel*. North Mankato, MN: Stone Arch Books, 2014.

Irving, Washington. *Rip Van Winkle*. Mankato, MN: Creative Education, 2011.

Websites

A Brief History of Tarrytown
www.tarrytowngov.com/about-tarrytown/pages/a-brief-history-of-tarrytown
Learn about the real Tarrytown and how it has grown since the time of the legend.

Ghost Stories
people.howstuffworks.com/culture-traditions/holidays-halloween/ghost-stories.htm
Read a version of the Sleepy Hollow legend and compare it to other ghost stories.

Index